Contents

Even as someone who is really keen on keeping domestic rats as pets, it is not difficult to see why they have got such bad press over the years. Spreading diseases such as bubonic plague, and destroying enormous amounts of stored grain is hardly the way to endear yourself to the human race. And that tail! It may be very useful to the rat, helping it to balance and grip when it is climbing, but there is something about its cold, snake-like quality that sends a shudder down many a spine.

But although they appear very similar, the domestic rat is a very different beast to its wild cousin. Domestic rats have been bred entirely separately from wild rats to give them a much more placid nature, and they do not have the opportunity to pick up the diseases that wild rats can carry.

The rat's tail gives it a tremendous sense of balance.

Wild rats should never be taken into captivity, or even handled unnecessarily, but domestic rats are extremely good pets.

The aim of this book is to persuade you that,

despite many people's natural revulsion, the rat is arguably the best of all the small mammals to be kept as a pet. It will also provide you with the information you need to purchase, rear, and even breed pet rats.

What Is A Rodent?

Rats belong to the rodent group of mammals. Like all mammals, they are warm-blooded and have a hairy skin. Females give birth to and rear live young, feeding them on their milk. Nearly fifty per cent of all the species of mammals are rodents, named after the Latin word rodere, meaning 'to gnaw'. This is because all rodents have one pair of upper and one pair of lower incisor teeth at the front of their mouth that grow continually and wear against each other as they gnaw at their food.

A most unusual cat – generally it is not a good idea to keep rats and cats in the same house.

?

Understanding Rats

Rats seem to have a particular affinity with humans, and seek them out for companionship. They are highly intelligent animals, and people who keep more than one notice that they develop their own personalities. Of course, cats and small dogs such as terriers are predators that have been bred to kill rodents, and unless they have grown up together, it is very unlikely that they will be safe in the same house.

DID YOU KNOW?

A rat's incisor teeth will grow approximately five inches each year.

Pet Rats

The more you handle your rat, the tamer it will become.

As with any pet, it is important to think about the time, effort and expense that is needed to look after your pet for the whole of its life. Fortunately, the rat is a pretty low-maintenance pet that does not make too many demands on its owner.

Perhaps one of the main disadvantages of rats is their relatively short life span–most live for just three or four years. Losing a pet is always tough – even if you know that life expectancy is short – but at least you can have the satisfaction of knowing that you have given your rat the best possible love and care.

Handling A Rat

It is important that rats are handled regularly and gently from an early age, as they will then become very tame. Pick up a rat by sliding your hand under its belly and then lifting its whole body. Do not pick it up by its tail, as you can damage the skin over it, and most rats, not surprisingly, resent being handled in this way.

If you need to keep you rat still for examination or treatment, you can grasp it gently but firmly over the shoulders, with your thumb under its neck to prevent it from biting.

Unlike many other species of animal that have been domesticated, all pet rats maintain the same basic body shape, but a wide range of coat colours have been bred. These colours can be classified into two mains groups:-

Solid colours

The body colour can be dark-brown, black, chocolate, grey, lavender (a light bluish grey), yellow, sand and silver. In addition, albino rats have been bred with no body pigment at all, so they have a white coat and pink eyes.

Spotted colours

These rats have patches of pigment on their body. The commonest variety is the hooded rat, with a white body, a dark head and shoulders, with a dark stripe extending down the back. Notched rats have a smaller hood and no stripe down the back, and Irish rats are white with coloured on their chest and belly.

Breeds Of Rat

Himalayan

Himalayan rats have now been bred with a light body colour and dark points on the nose and paws, and like a Siamese cat, the darkness of the points at the extremities depends upon the temperature difference – the lower the temperature, the darker the colour. Again, similarly to cats, rats have been bred with curly rex coats, and this coat type also comes in a variety of colours.

The Himalayan has a light body colour with dark points on the nose and paws.

DID YOU KNOW?

There are many species of rat around the world, living in many different environments. These include the high-jumping kangaroo rat from North America, the South American fish-eating rat, and the African spiny tree rat.

There is very little difference between the varieties of domestic rat from the point of view of keeping them as pets. The choice is therefore very much one of personal preference, although the depth of your pocket should also be taken into account, as the more unusual ones will be more expensive.

Most reputable pet shops sell rats, and the best will be able to offer you advice on what to buy. Alternatively, you may know someone locally who breeds and possibly competes at shows, and might be able to help. Your veterinary surgeon may know of a breeder, or you may be able to obtain a pet from a friend who has bred some.

A pair of rats will keep each other company.

In all instances, look for a rat that is clean and well cared-for. In a pet shop, it is a good sign if the staff are knowledgeable and can give you

advice when you are making your choice. Resist the temptation of buying a sickly rat from a pet shop just because you feel sorry for it – you could end up a lot of heartache, trouble and expense trying to get it well.

It is best to buy pet rats at about a month old because they are much easier to socialise and train at this age.

How Many?

If you are just going to keep one rat, then the sex is not important. However, it is probably better to keep a pair, so that they can keep each other

DID YOU KNOW?

There are two important species of wild rat found in Europe, Rattus rattus, the black rat, and Rattus norwegicus, the larger brown rat, which is the likely ancestor of our domestic rat. Brown rats are more often found living above ground level, and are therefore also known as roof rats.

company when you are not around. Two rats introduced to each other before they become sexually mature will usually get on fine together, so you can either keep a same-sex pair, or one of each sex. Of course, in the latter case the pair will start to breed, and you will need to think about finding good homes for the offspring, having them neutered, or finding larger premises!

What Sex Is My Rat?

Rats sexually mature at around two months of age, and at that stage it is easy to tell the sexes apart. The male has very obvious testicles which can be seen in the scrotal sac protruding from the body behind the anus. Even when young, rats can be sexed fairly reliably, with a little experience, as the males have a much greater distance separating the genital opening from the anus, and in the females a line of nipples can be seen along the tummy.

Male.

Female.

SKIN:
Pink and clear
ears and tail

BEHAVIOUR:
Active and alert

The Signs Of A Healthy Rat

The rat should have a good appetite, and you should look in the cage to ensure you can see well-formed droppings.

Check for the following signs of good health:

COAT:
Well groomed. Should not be soiled or matted

BODY CONDITION:
Well covered and rounded. No abnormal swellings

EYES: Bright and clear, without any discharge

NOSE:
Clean and free of discharge

BREATHING:
Quiet and regular. Should not be laboured

MOUTH: Clean. Dribbling can be a sign of problems

Buying A Rat

DID YOU KNOW?

Rodents range in size from the tiny Old World harvest mouse at around 4 grams, to the South American capybara at a massive 40 kg – about ten thousand times heavier!

The Journey Home

You will need to transport your rat in a suitable carrier with some paper shavings for comfort. Small, plastic pet carriers can be purchased quite cheaply, designed rather like a small cat carrier, with a close-fitting lid and pierced by ventilation holes.

Introducing A New Rat

If you purchase a new rat to add to an existing group, you should always keep it in strict isolation for a couple of weeks to make sure it is not incubating any diseases before you introduce it to the others. It is then best to introduce them to each other on neutral territory.

If you are introducing a new rat, keep it in isolation for the first couple of weeks.

Plan ahead and have the housing set up at home before you purchase a new rat.

An Ideal Home

There is nothing rats like more than a nice piece of wood to chew on, so wooden cages are really not suitable. Wire cages are often used, but they are not ideal either. The best home for one or two pet rats is a glass aquarium with a wire-mesh top – that will either need to clip on to the top of the tank, or be weighted in place with a brick or something of a similar weight.

A tank that is 24 x 12 x 12ins (70 x 35 x 35cms) will be large enough for a couple of small rats, but a larger tank will give them more room for exercise and allow for growth.

Wire cages are often used for rats.

Siting The Tank

Position the tank or cage away from open windows or direct sunlight, as rats dislike draughts and can easily suffer from heat-stroke if overheated, which can happen particularly easily in a glass tank. Rats also prefer relatively subdued light levels, particularly albino rats, which lack pigment in the iris.

The ideal home is a well-ventilated aquarium with a secure cover.

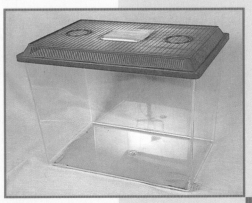

Rats

also like a relatively humid environment (between 40 and 70 per cent saturation), although it should not become excessively damp. The environmental temperature should be kept between 65 and 85 degrees Fahrenheit (18-29C); warmer temperatures predispose rats to respiratory problems and even heatstroke.

Floor Covering

The floor of the tank can be covered with a couple of inches of wood shavings, which the rats will enjoy rummaging around in. It is important that the shavings do not come from wood that has been treated with any preservatives. Shredded paper is also fine. A toilet area should be allocated away from food and bedding.

Food Bowls

Heavy ceramic food bowls are preferable, as they cannot be chewed like plastic, and are heavy enough not to be turned over.

Ladders And Platforms

Rats appreciate a selection of
platforms at various heights.
They are good climbers, and
will make use of ladders
and wooden climbing
frames, although
this may include
eating them!

Water Bottle

Rats do not generally drink very
much, especially if they eat
significant amounts of succulent
foods such as fruit and
vegetables, but they should
always have a supply of fresh
water available. This is best
supplied by a gravity-fed
drinking water bottle that can
be suspended upside down in
the cage or tank.

DID YOU KNOW?

The oldest recorded
pet rat was Rodney,
named after his
owner, Rodney
Mitchell of Oklahoma,
USA, who died at the
age of seven years
and four months

A wide range of rat toys and food treats are available, but they should be selected with care. Wooden blocks with hidey-holes appeal to the tunnelling instincts of rats and are much appreciated. You can even use a series of wooden blocks to construct a maze for your pet rat, with a food reward at the end. You will discover that they will quickly memorise their way through them.

Most rats also enjoy swimming, and you can provide a shallow tub for them to swim in, under supervision, making sure there is a large rock in the tub for them to climb on to when they tire.

Sometimes the cheapest toys are the best − so try giving your rat a present of the cardboard tube from inside a toilet roll, which they will thoroughly enjoy investigating and then chewing up.

Running Free

Letting a pet rodent have free run of the house is a recipe for disaster, as they can easily get lost or injured, and love sharpening their teeth on electrical flex. However, they can be brought out of their home for regular exercise under supervision.

Training

Don't pounce on the new arrival as soon as you get it home – let the rat settle down alone in its cage with a supply of fresh food and water before you start hand-taming it. Even if you move its home later on, initially it should be situated in a quiet spot, away from hustle and bustle.

Get the rat used to the scent of your hand, and then tempt it with tasty treats to come to you. Rats learn quickly, and will soon come running to greet you, particularly if you start off feeding them entirely by hand.

Rats are quick witted and will soon learn to enjoy human companionship.

DID YOU KNOW?

Rats do not have very good vision, and are not able to see great detail or differing colours. However, they are very good at judging distances, and have excellent senses of touch (with the aid of their whiskers) and smell.

Feeding

The ideal balanced food for pet rats is one of the complete diets that are designed to provide all their nutritional needs. Because rats are commonly kept as laboratory animals, where it is essential that they receive a well-balanced diet, a lot of work has gone into producing complete pelleted foods for rats. These may seem boring, but they do ensure that the rat cannot just pick out the morsels he fancies and leave the rest.

Make some hay available to provide some extra fibre. Don't buy more than a couple of months supply of food, and keep it in a dry, air-tight container.

Complete feeds supply the basic needs.

A Rat Feast

Complete foods may supply the basic needs of pet rats, but a variety of food provides interest for both the animal and its owner, since we all get enjoyment from seeing the pleasure that a special treat may give. Over the page are some of the things your rat may safely tuck into. However, they should not make up more than 10 per cent of the total diet.

Feeding

Seeds and nuts: leave in the shell.

Apple: a bit of fruit is appreciated from time to time.

Greens and carrots: preferably not lettuce or celery.

Wholemeal toast: go very easy on the butter.

Hard-boiled egg, cheese, meat scraps: just a little from time to time, especially when rearing young.

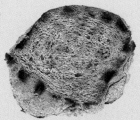

Supplements

If you are giving your rat a varied diet, or a complete food that has been well made up, there should be no need to add extra vitamins and minerals to the diet. If you are concerned that your pet may not be getting enough of these, especially at times when they need extra, such as when they are growing, or rearing their young, a tiny pinch of a balanced small animal supplement can be sprinkled on to the food a couple of times a week.

Caring For Your Rat

There are no vaccinations that you can give your rat to prevent diseases, in the way that you can with pet cats and dogs. Fortunately, rats have few health problems, and as long as you provide them with suitable food and housing, as described in this book, ailments are rare.

Cleaning The Tank

Rats will generally select a toilet area, which can be cleaned on a daily basis. The whole cage or tank should be thoroughly cleaned and disinfected every week or two.

Teeth

A rat's teeth grow all the time, but normally wear down naturally if there are plenty of things to gnaw on. A wooden block or a fruit tree branch (that hasn't been sprayed with insecticides) will help to keep the teeth in trim. Sometimes the teeth do not develop in proper alignment and become over-grown. If this happens, the rat

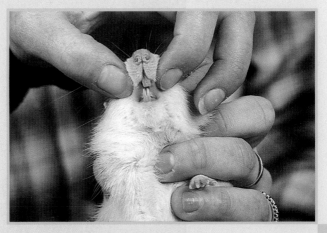

A rat's teeth grow all the time, and are worn down by gnawing.

will show signs of discomfort around its mouth and they may then need regular cutting.

Nails

Rats generally keep their toenails short by digging and scrabbling around their cage. However, you should check them from time to time to ensure they do not need clipping, especially if the rat is elderly. It is best to get a vet to show you how to clip nails and teeth. Nail-clipping can then be carried out at home, using nail clippers. If you are a novice rat-keeper, ask someone more experienced to help. Cutting a nail too short will be painful and cause bleeding, although this will soon stop if left alone.

Nails may need to be trimmed, but this should be done by your vet or an experienced rat-keeper.

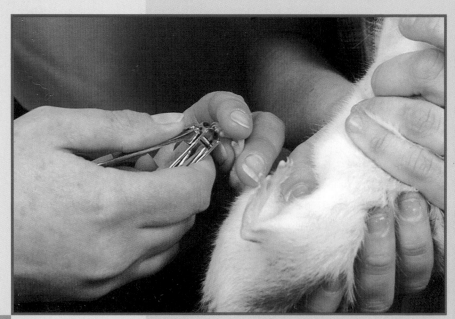

Breeding

There is not a great deal you need to do to arrange for a pair of rats to breed, and if there are more than one pair together, they will not form pairs, but mate with different males at different times. A female rat will come into heat every four or five days, and accept a male for mating for a period of about 24 hours. There is no 'breeding season' for rats, and they will mate and produce young at any time of year. In breeding colonies, one male is often kept with between two and six females, as he takes no part in rearing the young.

Pregnancy lasts about three weeks, and a pregnant female should be removed to her own quarters a few days before she is due to give birth, as the males sometimes attack the young. Females will build a nest from their bedding material, and usually gives birth to somewhere between six and twelve young. The nesting cage should be kept comfortably warm, between 70 and 80 degrees Fahrenheit (around 24C).

DID YOU KNOW?

Rats have a sweet tooth, and this can be used to tempt a sickly rat to eat. Sugar-coated cereals are one of the best ways to get some energy into a rat that won't eat.

The young are born hairless, and they are unable to see or hear.

The First Few Days

The youngsters are born extremely immature, with no hair and unable to hear or see, but they develop quickly. They are weaned and ready to leave the nest by three weeks of age. Mum needs very little human assistance during this stage, and interfering with her nest could cause her to eat her young. Just ensure she has a highly nutritious diet.

The female will come into heat again within about 48 hours of giving birth, and can have another litter immediately. However, this is a considerable drain on her resources, and it is best to allow her to rest for a while. Females enter menopause and become infertile at about 15 months of age.

DID YOU KNOW?

Rat baiting was a popular sport in this country a couple of hundred years ago, where rats were placed in a pit along with a ferocious terrier. Spectators placed bets on how long it would take the dog to kill every rat. Of course, this so-called sport is illegal now.

Rats

can be left for a couple of days, so long as there is a good supply of food and water. Only a small amount of perishable food, such as fruit and green vegetables, should be left. If you need to be away for a longer period, you may be able to board your rat with a vet, a pet shop, or perhaps a breeder. Of course, a rat is small enough to be moved easily to a friend or relative that may be prepared to look after it, or a neighbour may be prepared to make a daily check for feeding and cleaning.

Make sure that whoever looks after your rat knows all about its requirements, and leave the contact number of your veterinary surgeon in case a problem should arise.

Do not leave your rat on its own for more than a couple of days.

First Aid

The most important care for a sick or injured rat is to keep it warm and administer fluids to try and prevent dehydration, which can occur quite quickly. A dropper or a small syringe is ideal for administering solutions, but do not use excessive force. Fluids can cause more harm than good if they are inhaled.

Commercial rehydration powders, that are designed to be made up with water, can be purchased from a vet or a chemist – but a rat will only take a few drops at a time. Alternatively, you can use boiled tap-water that has been allowed to cool, with a heaped tablespoonful of glucose powder and a level teaspoonful of salt added per pint (450 mls).

Small wounds can be gently flushed with warm water and treated with a mild antiseptic, but any major injuries will require veterinary attention. It is quite common for an over-inquisitive rat to fall off a high surface. If this happens, the rat should be gently returned to its nest to recover from the shock. If it is not improving within an hour, it may have broken some bones or suffered internal injuries, and will need to see a vet. Make sure you have a small, plastic pet carrier to hand for this purpose.

Going To The Vet

If your rat is seriously unwell, your veterinary surgeon must be contacted without delay for assistance. Although children often care for rats, it is necessary for a responsible adult to take the rat along and authorise any treatment needed.

Most small animal veterinary practices see a large number of small mammals and are very willing and able to treat them. It is even possible to anaesthetise rats to carry out surgical operations, such as tumour removal or surgical neutering, and modern techniques make these procedures relatively safe even in a creature as small as a rat.

Treating rats

There are few products that have been developed and tested for use in rats, because the market is simply not big enough to make it financially viable for a drug company. Therefore a vet has to use products that are available for use

DID YOU KNOW?

Rats are believed to be the living representatives of the Hindu goddess Karniji, and a temple in Deshnok, India, is dedicated to them. Its marble walls have Tom-and-Jerry style mouseholes for the rodents to live, and predators are kept strictly out. Over 10,000 brown rats live in the temple, sharing their food with worshippers. They are totally unafraid of humans, even eating from the same plates. The people of Deshnok village believe they will be reincarnated as rats when they die.

in other species of animal, or even human medicines. This makes the use of any drug more unpredictable in rats than in many other animals.

Dosing a rat with medicine can be difficult, although it can sometimes be managed with drops of a liquid medicine that can be given orally or added to some food. A rat may refuse to drink water that has been treated, particularly when it is unwell. A course of injections is often the safest way to ensure a rat does receive a proper course of treatment, but does involve repeated visits to the vet.

DID YOU KNOW?

Rats become sexually mature at between just seven and nine weeks of age, and have been known to bear young at just 65 days of age.

Common Ailments

There are a wide range of diseases that have been reported in rats, but very few of them are common in those kept in small groups as pets. Those of most importance include:-

Respiratory disease ●————————

Respiratory infections are common, and underlying causes can include poor ventilation, dusty cage bedding, or dirty flooring that holds in ammonia from the rat's urine.

All rats have a range of potentially harmful bacteria and viruses in their lungs, but their immune system keeps them under control. However, they get a chance to multiply and cause disease problems if the rat's natural resistance is lowered by poor hygiene, inadequate diet, illness, injury, or just old age. The rat will show signs of sneezing, red and watery eyes, and laboured breathing

Treatment with antibiotics may help the problem, particularly if only the upper airways are affected, but it is often more a matter of control rather than cure. The outlook for a rat with pneumonia (infection of the lungs) is very poor.

Common Ailments

Diarrhoea

This is another common condition affecting pet rats. It can be due to a variety of causes, such as infection with bacteria, protozoa (single-celled organisms), or parasites such as roundworms and tapeworms. Sudden changes in diet, or the feeding of food that has gone rancid or mouldy, can also spark off a digestive upset.

Mild cases will often respond to conservative treatment, removing all perishable foodstuffs from the diet and simply feeding a complete, dry food. In more serious or longer lasting cases, a veterinary surgeon may want to have a faecal sample analysed to try and establish the cause.

Occasionally, rats can be infected with an organism that can be passed on to people, such as salmonella, commonly associated with human food poisoning. Strict hygiene, including keeping pet rats away from food preparation areas and hand-washing after handling, is always advisable, but particularly so in the case of a rat showing signs of digestive disturbance.

Skin problems

Infectious skin problems are not common in rats kept as pets, because they generally have very little opportunity to come into contact with other rats. It is possible for them to suffer from ringworm, a fungus that grows on the hairs and can also cause skin problems in

---

DID YOU KNOW?

The rat is notorious for having helped spread bubonic plague, the cause of the Black Death that wreaked havoc in the 14th century, although it was actually the rat's fleas that spread the disease.

humans and other animals. This is usually seen a patches of hair loss with scaliness of the underlying skin, especially around the head.

Rats can also be affected by mites, which either live on the surface of the skin or burrow deeper into it. These tend to cause quite a lot of irritation, and can be diagnosed by a vet by taking a scraping from the skin.

In the case of either fungal or parasitic infections of the skin, it is usually necessary for a vet to prescribe a medicated shampoo for treatment.

Cancer

This is very common in older rats, occurring in many possible sites around the body. Mammary (breast) cancer is particularly frequently seen, but surprisingly, breast tissue can be found over most of the body, so breast cancer can even appear as a lump on the back of the rat! Some non-malignant growths can be removed surgically.

Ear disease

Although rats do not often get infections of the outer part of the ear canal, it is not uncommon for them

to suffer from an infection of the inner part of the ear, which will affect their balance, causing head tilt, circling and loss of balance.

Treatment with antibiotics is successful in some cases, but they are often left with a permanent head tilt. Fortunately, most rats are able to adapt to this relatively minor handicap and live a normal life.

Ringtail

If young rats are kept at very low humidity levels, the blood vessels may constrict and cut off the vascular supply to the tail. This will then result in gangrene in the part of the tail behind the constricted vessels, and that part of the tail will often drop off. Fortunately, the stump usually heals without complications.

Eye problems

Conjunctivitis is not uncommon in rats causing soreness of the eyes. It can be sparked off by a more generalised illness such as a respiratory infection, or by irritation of the eyes by dust particles. A veterinary surgeon will be able to prescribe an antibiotic ointment to treat the problem.

When stressed, rats sometimes excrete substances called porphyrins into the tears. These substances are a reddish colour, and make may the tears look blood-stained.

Poisoning ●————

Rats are quite sensitive to poisoning, particularly because they spend a lot of time grooming and will lick off any substances that get on to the coat. Take great care not to use any aerosol sprays in the room in which the rat lives without checking first to make sure they are non-toxic to animals.